The beginning is half of the whole.

      – Plato (c. 428–348 B.C.)
      Greek philosopher

20 19

Digit on the right indicates the number of this printing.

ISBN 1-56138-066-0

Cover design by Toby Schmidt
Cover illustration by Antonio Peticov
courtesy of John Szoke Graphics Inc., New York, NY.
Interior design by Christian Benton

This book may be ordered by mail from the publisher.
Please add $2.50 for postage and handling.
But try your bookstore first!
Running Press Book Publishers
125 South Twenty-second Street
Philadelphia, Pennsylvania 19103-4399

NEW BEGINNINGS

RUNNING PRESS
PHILADELPHIA · LONDON

In the middle of difficulty lies opportunity.

- **Albert Einstein** (1879-1955)
German-born American physicist

All rising to great places is by a winding stair.

- Francis Bacon (1561-1626)
English philosopher and writer

Men must be decided on what they will not do, and

then they are able to act with vigor on what they

ought to do.

- **Mencius** (c. 371-c. 289 B.C.)
Chinese philosopher

A pile of rocks ceases to be a rock pile when somebody

contemplates it with the idea of a cathedral in mind.

- Antoine de Saint-Exupéry (1900-1944)
French writer and aviator

The fact is, nothing comes; at least nothing good.

All has to be fetched.

- **Charles Buxton** (1823-1871)
English writer

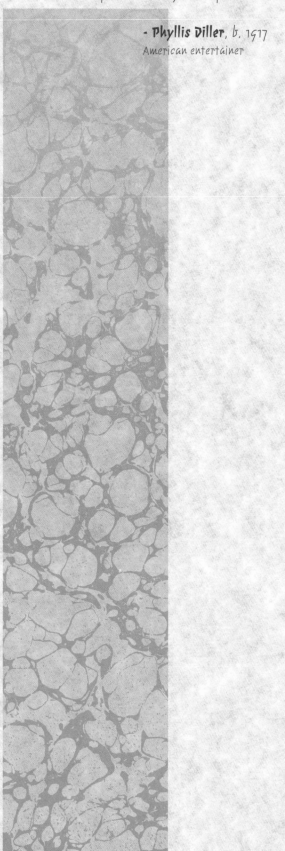

Life is a do-it-yourself kit.

- Phyllis Diller, b. 1917
American entertainer

Put a grain of boldness into everything you do.

— **Baltasar Gracian** (1601-1658)
Spanish writer

Risk! Risk anything! Care no more for the opinions

of others, for those voices. Do the hardest thing

on earth for you. Act for yourself.

- **Katherine Mansfield** (1888-1923)
New Zealand-born English writer

It does not take much strength to do things,

but it requires great strength to decide on

what to do.

— Elbert Hubbard (1856-1915)
American writer and editor

You can do what you have to do, and sometimes

you can do it even better than you think you can.

— Jimmy Carter, b. 1924
39th U.S. President

It is right to be contented with what we have,

never with what we are.

- **Sir James Mackintosh** (1765-1832)
Scottish statesman and historian

Once you say you're going to settle for second,

that's what happens to you in life, I find.

- John F. Kennedy (1917-1963)
35th U.S. President

You only grow by coming to the end of something

and by beginning something else.

- John Irving, b. 1942
American writer

Bring ideas in and entertain them royally,

for one of them may be the king.

- **Mark van Doren** (1894-1972)
American writer and editor

Man's mind stretched to a new idea never goes

back to its original dimensions.

- **Oliver Wendell Holmes, Sr.** (1809-1894)
American poet and writer

Some minds seem almost to create themselves,

springing up under every disadvantage and

working their solitary but irresistible way

through a thousand obstacles.

- Washington Irving (1783-1859)
American writer

A great deal of talent is lost in this world for want of a little courage.

- Sydney Smith (1771-1845)
English essayist and clergyman

It is best . . . to act with confidence no matter

how little right you have to it.

- **Lillian Hellman** (1906-1984)
American writer and playwright

Don't be afraid to take big steps. You can't

cross a chasm in two small jumps.

- **David Lloyd George** (1863-1945)
English statesman

I hate to see things done by halves. If it

be right, do it boldly . . . .

- Bernard Gilpin (1517-1583)
English clergyman

Ideas won't keep; something must be done about them.

- **Alfred North Whitehead** (1861-1947)
English philosopher and mathematician

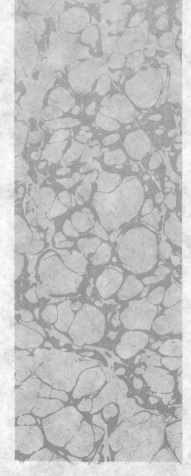

Seize the moment of excited curiosity on any

subject to solve your doubts; for if you let it

pass, the desire may never return . . . .

– **William Wirt** (1772–1834)
American lawyer

There is no such thing as a long piece of work,

except one that you dare not start.

- Charles Baudelaire (1821-1867)
French poet

He who is outside the door has already a good

part of his journey behind him,

— Dutch proverb

The bravest thing you can do when you are not

brave is to profess courage and act accordingly.

- Corra May White Harris (1869-1935)
American writer

I don't know which takes more courage:

surviving a lifelong endurance test because

you once made a promise or breaking free,

disrupting all your world.

– Anne Tyler, b. 1941
American writer

When you get in a tight place and everything

goes against you, till it seems as though you

could not hold on a minute longer, never give

up then, for that is just the place and time

that the tide will turn.

- **Harriett Beecher Stowe** (1811-1896)
American writer

. . . remember this maxim: Attacking is the only

secret. Dare and the world always yields; or if

it beats you sometimes, dare it again and it

will succumb.

- William M. Thackeray (1811-1863)
English writer

We're given second chances every day of our life.

We don't usually take them, but they're there for

the taking.

- Andrew M. Greeley, b. 1928
American writer

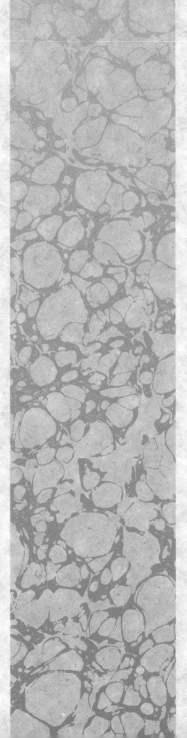

. . . don't worry about being worried. You're heading

out on an adventure and you can always change your

mind along the way and try something else.

- **Tracy Kidder**, b. 1945
American writer

There is nothing to be gained by wishing you were

someplace else or waiting for a better situation.

You see where you are and you do what you can

with that.

- **Jacob K. Javits** (1904-1986)
U.S. Senator

Tomorrow is the most important thing in life . . .

Comes into us at midnight very clean. It's perfect

when it arrives and it puts itself in our hands.

It hopes we've learned something from yesterday.

- John Wayne (1907-1979)
American actor

. . . Life is like a game of chess . . . there are many moves

possible, but each move determines your _next_ move . . .

where you wind up is the sum total of all your _past_

moves . . . but first you have to make _some_ kind of move.

— Mort Walker, b. 1929
American cartoonist

The first step.....is the one on which depends the rest.....

- **Voltaire** (1694-1778)
French writer

I am only one; but still I am one. I cannot do everything,

but still I can do something; I will not refuse to do the something

I can do.

- Helen Keller (1880-1968)
American writer

One has to choose in life.

— Grace Kelly (1929-1982)
American-born actress and Princess of Monaco

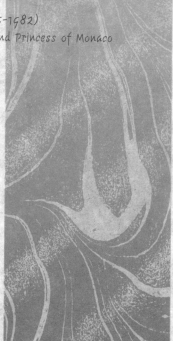

Experience is a hard teacher because she gives the test first, the lesson after.

- **Vernon Law**, b. 1930
American baseball player

To be happy, drop the words *if only* and

substitute instead the words *next time*.

- Smiley Blanton (1882-1966)
American physician

Bad times have a scientific value.....We learn geology the morning after the earthquake.

           – R.W. Emerson (1803-1882)
           American essayist and poet

Skilful pilots gain their reputation from storms and tempests.

- Epicurus (341-270 B.C.)
Greek philosopher

A thousand things advance; nine hundred and

ninety-nine retreat; that is progress.

- Henri Frédéric Amiel (1821-1881)
Swiss poet and philosopher

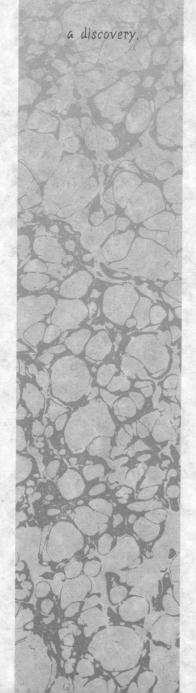

......He who never made a mistake never made

a discovery.

— **Samuel Smiles** (1812–1904)
English writer

If you're not making mistakes, you're not trying

hard enough.

- Allan R. Sandage, b. 1926
American cosmologist

It's never too late--in fiction or in life -- to revise.

- Nancy Thayer, b. 1943
American writer

For some reason, we see divorce as a signal of failure

despite the fact that each of us has a right and an

obligation to rectify any other mistake we make

in life.

- Joyce Brothers, b. 1929
American psychologist

...I don't consider my marriages as failures!

It's idiotic to assume that because a marriage

ends, it's failed.

– Margaret Mead (1901–1978)
American anthropologist and writer

.....if we insist upon being as sure as is conceivable,

in every step of our course, we must be content to

creep along the ground, and can never soar.

- **John Henry Newman** (1801-1890)
English theologian

You won't skid if you stay in a rut.

— **Kin Hubbard** (1868–1930)
American humorist and writer

It gives one a sense of freedom to know that anyone

in this world can really do a deliberately

courageous act.

- Henrik Ibsen (1828-1906)
Norwegian poet and playwright

Effort is only effort when it begins to hurt.

- Jose Ortega y Gasset (1883-1955)
Spanish philosopher and writer

Happiness is like a cat. If you try to coax it . . .

it will avoid you. It will never come.

But if you pay no attention to it and go about

your business, you'll find it rubbing against

your legs and jumping into your lap. So forget

pursuing happiness. Pin your hopes on work,

on family, on learning, on knowing, on loving.

Forget pursuing happiness; pursue these other

things and with luck happiness will come.

- **William Bennett**, b. 1943
Former U.S. secretary of education

Nothing is far and nothing is dear, if one

desires . . . There is only one big thing--desire.

And before it, when it is big, all is little.

- **Willa Cather** (1873-1947)
American writer

Luck and strength go together. When you get lucky,

you have to have the strength to follow through. You

also have to have the strength to wait for the luck.

- **Mario Puzo**, b. 1920
American writer

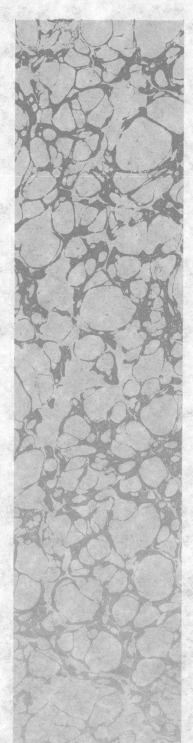

Remember that the faith that removes mountains

always carries a pick.

- Anonymous

Every day I wake up, I think, what a blessing --

I'm alive. I don't care if it snows, it rains, it

thunderstorms--a heatwave, I think, I'm here--

this is terrific.

- Richard Harris, b. 1930
Irish actor

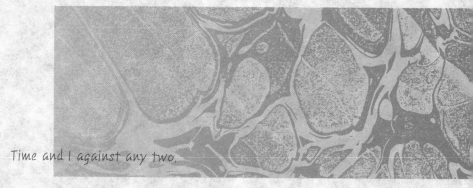

Time and I against any two.

 - Spanish proverb

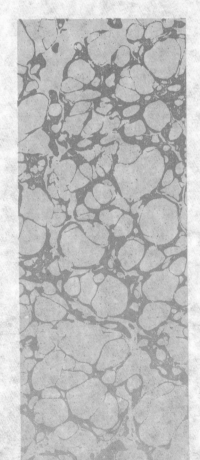

Before you begin, consider well; and when you

have considered, act.

- Sallust (86-34 B.C.)
Roman historian

The most absurd and reckless aspirations have

sometimes led to extraordinary success.

- M. de Vauvenargues (1715-1747)
French soldier and moralist

The world is round and the place which may seem

like the end may also be only the beginning.

- **Ivy Baker Priest** (1905-1975)
U.S. Treasurer

Never cut what you can untie.

- Joseph Joubert (1754-1824)
French essayist

Survival, I know, is to begin again.

- Judy Collins, b. 1939
American singer and songwriter

Begin to weave and God will give the thread.

— German proverb

When all else is lost, the future still remains.

— **Christian Nestell Bovee** (1820-1904)
American writer

Hope is an echo, hope ties itself yonder, yonder.

- Carl Sandburg (1878-1967)
American poet

. . . when you're feeling helpless and hopeless,

the worst thing you can do is just stand back

and let people rescue you.

- Linda Henley, b. 1951
American writer

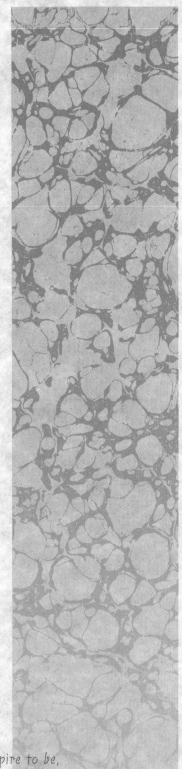

What we truly and earnestly aspire to be,

that in some sense we are.

- Anna Brownell Jameson (1794-1860)
Irish writer

The absurd man is the one who never changes.

     - Auguste M. Barthelemy (1796-1867)
     French poet

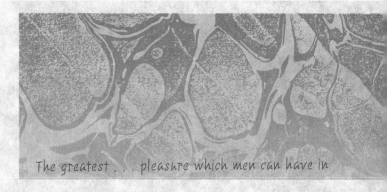

The greatest . . . pleasure which men can have in

this world is to discover new truths; and the

next is to shake off old prejudices.

- **Frederick the Great** (1620-1688)
Elector of Brandenburg

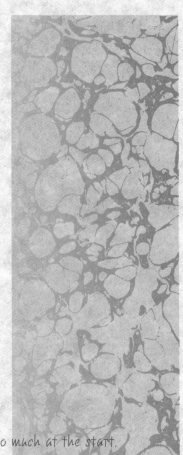

Beware of undertaking too much at the start.

Be content with quite a little. Allow for accidents.

Allow for human nature, especially your own.

- **Arnold Bennett** (1867-1931)
English writer

... always prepare secondary ways of dealing with problems.

- **Frank Herbert** (1920-1968)
American writer

. . . you always have two ways to run. Away from . . .

or towards . . .

- Joe Gores, b. 1937
American writer

Face it. Face it, and it'll vanish.

– Evan Hunter, b. 1926
American writer

No question is so difficult to answer as that to

which the answer is obvious.

- George Bernard Shaw (1856-1950)
English playwright

A problem is never as permanent as a solution.

- **Harvey Fierstein**, b. 1954
American playwright and actor

Let us watch well our beginnings, and results will

manage themselves.

- Alexander Clark (1834-1879)
American clergyman

All beginnings are somewhat strange; but we must

have patience, and, little by little, we shall find

things, which at first were obscure, becoming clear.

- Vincent De Paul (c. 1580-1660)
French missionary

Few things are impossible of themselves;

application to make them succeed fails us

more often than the means.

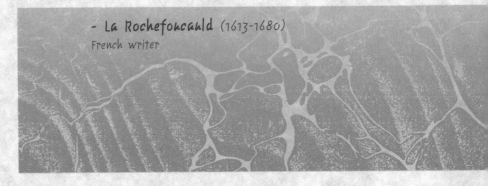

- La Rochefoucauld (1613-1680)
French writer

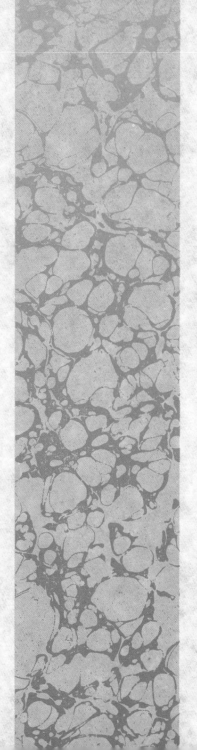

Even if you're on the right track, you'll get run

over if you just sit there.

- Will Rogers (1879-1935)
American writer, humorist, and actor

There is nothing more difficult to take in
hand.....than.....the introduction of a new order
of things.

- Niccolò Machiavelli (1469-1527)
Italian statesman and philosopher

Confusion is a word we have invented for an

order which is not understood.

- Henry Miller (1891-1980)
American writer

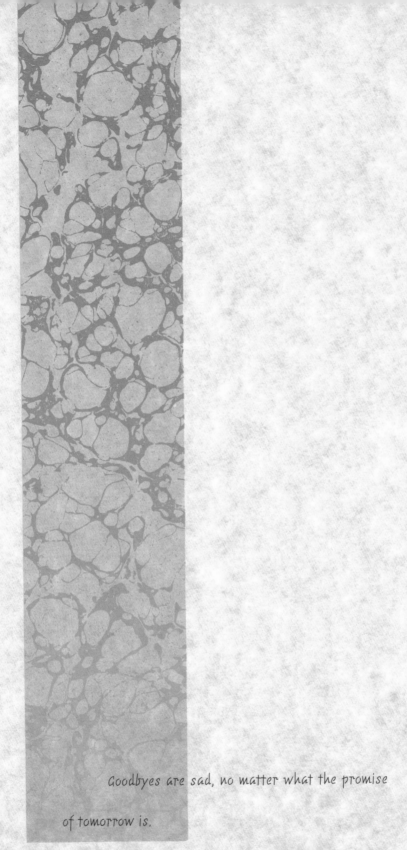

Goodbyes are sad, no matter what the promise

of tomorrow is.

— Janet Leigh, b. 1927
American actress

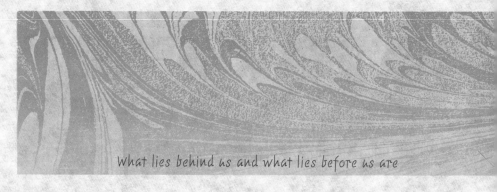

What lies behind us and what lies before us are

tiny matters compared with what lies within us.

- Anonymous

My parents, my teachers, my friends, my ex-wife--

everybody held up a mirror and I accepted the image

that came back. Well, it finally dawned on me that

my reflection in others' eyes was the truth

once removed.

- **Richard Moran**, b. 1942
American writer

Self-confidence is the first requisite to

great undertakings.

- **Samuel Johnson** (1709-1784)
English writer

. . . there are insights to be learned at the bottom

of the ladder.

- Jonathan Kellerman, b. 1949
American writer

If you don't get everything you want, think of

the things you don't get that you don't want.

- Oscar Wilde (1854-1900)
Irish poet and playwright

One is daily annoyed by some little corner that

needs clearing up and when by accident one at

last is stirred to do the needful, one wonders

that one should have stood the annoyance so long

when such a little effort would have done away

with it. Moral: When in doubt, do it.

- Oliver Wendell Holmes, Jr. (1841-1935)
American jurist

Never put off until tomorrow what you can

do today, because if you enjoy it today, you

can do it again tomorrow.

- Anonymous

We need courage to throw away old garments

which have had their day . . .

- Fridtjof Nansen (1861-1930)
Norwegian explorer and statesman

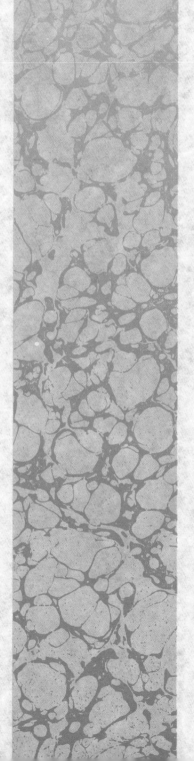

Only begin and then the mind grows heated,

Only begin and the task will be completed.

- J.W. von Goethe (1749-1832)
German poet

The fishermen know that the sea is dangerous

and the storm terrible, but they have never

found these dangers sufficient reason for

remaining ashore.

- **Vincent van Gogh** (1853-1890)
Dutch painter

Life is ours to be spent, not to be saved.

- D.H. Lawrence (1885-1930)
English writer

Begin to be now what you will be hereafter.

- Saint Jerome (c. 340-420)
Latin scholar